This book is all about Toy Grade RC car restoration and conversion to "real RC". Remember the 80s where we had Taiyo, Nikko and Bandai producing RC buggies giving us endless hours of fun and enjoyment? After 30+ years these RC cars are seriously aged. For them to run again a lot of things have to be fixed. And the electronics are likely dead already so you may as well go the real RC route by using real RC car electronics on them.

This book shows you how these can be accomplished using real life examples. Two Taiyo (Tyco that is) 1:12 RWD buggies are being used to showcase the modifications necessary to turn toy grade cars into real RC cars.

Video reviews of these cars are available at Toys-REVIEW.NET:

http://toys-review.net/2017/02/04/taiyo-jet-fighter-rc/

http://toys-review.net/2021/02/04/vintage-taiyo-rcs-upgraded/

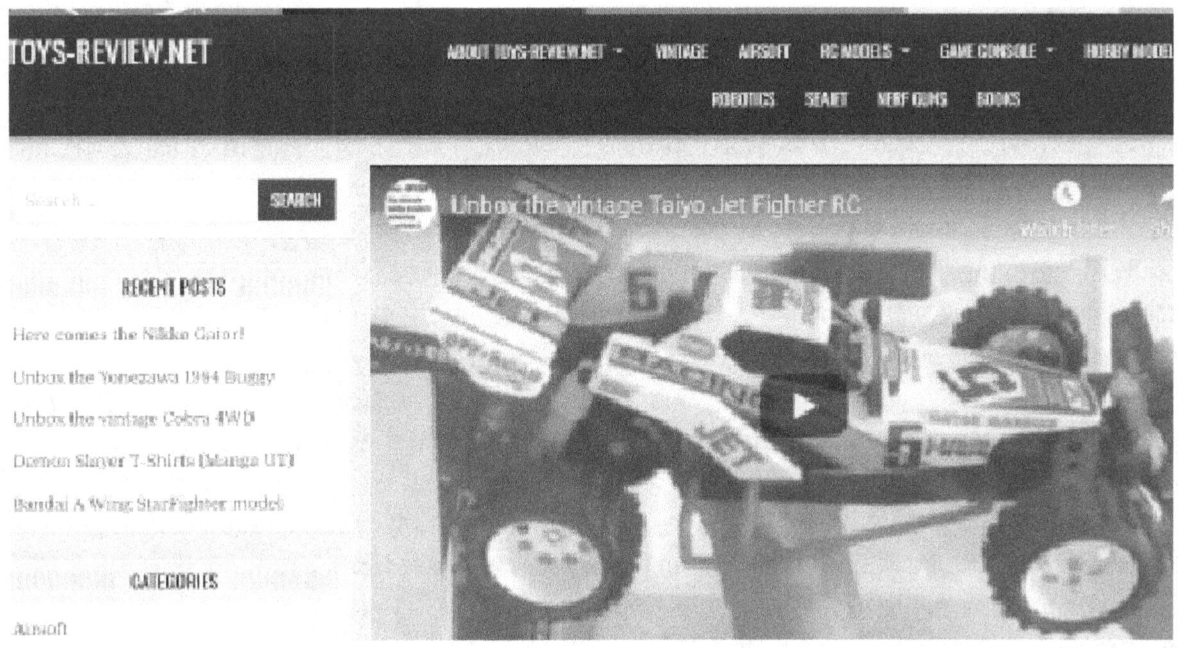

TABLE OF CONTENTS

This book (the "Book") is a product provided by RC PRESS o/b AirsoftPRESS (being referred to as "RCPRESS" in this document).

You may not modify the Book or create any derivative work of the Book or its accompanying documentation. Derivative works include but are not limited to translations.

You may not copy any part of the Book unless formal written authorization is obtained from us.

RCPRESS will not be held liable for any advice or suggestions given in this book. If the reader wants to follow a suggestion, it is at his or her own discretion. Suggestions are only offered to help.

PREFACE

R.C.PRESS is the premier information source for RC technologies. It has the goal of putting all different kinds of RC technologies on the global map by publishing e-books that bring to light the knowledge of RC technology innovators.

Members of the R.C.PRESS editorial team are practicing engineers, technicians and racers who have been with RC since the 80s. Being geographically close to the origin of RC products enables close contact with the major manufacturers, thus facilitating accurate coverage of the technologies. Because we are part of the industry, we know what information is really needed, and we make sure our books tell what people really need to know. We do not mind to criticize things that don't work, and we will not hesitate to give you hacks and workarounds to difficult problems. Reading this book should be like having a RC professional by your side, passing on useful hints whenever you get stuck.

Throughout the book we include references to our free RC infoAPPs. You can use these apps for free via the link under "Publications" of our website:

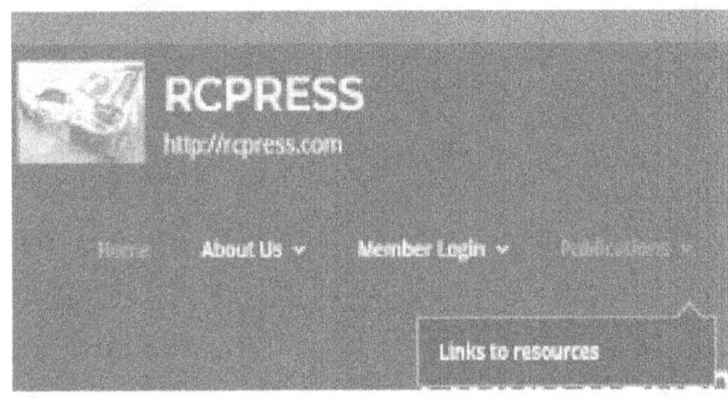

OVERVIEW

The photo below shows a Jet Fighter Twin Turbo. It shows the basic components such as the bumper, the spoilers (there are two on this car), the dampers and the wheels.

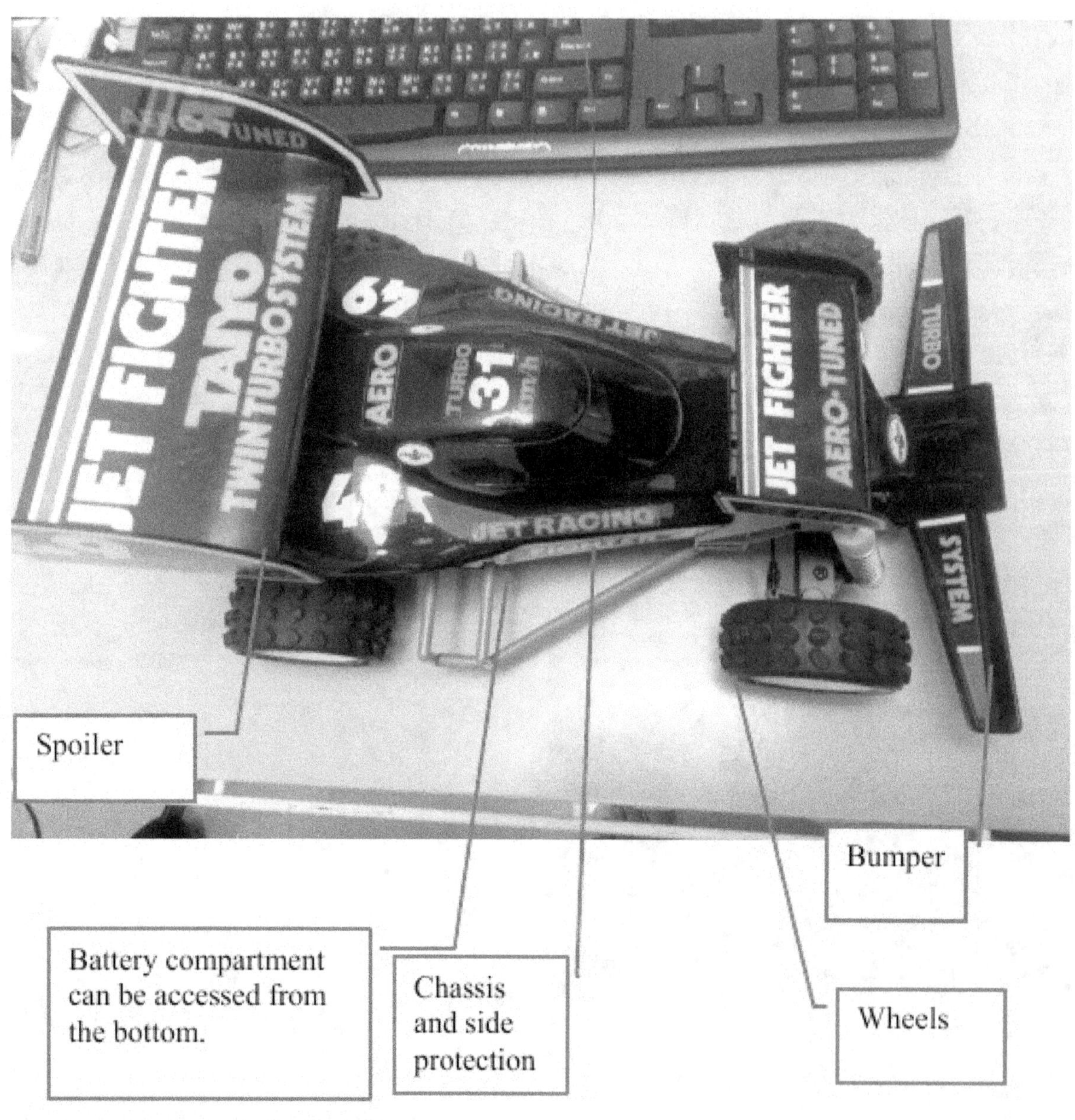

The picture above shows a standard version Jet Hopper. It has all the critical inside components of a typical toy grade RC car. The electronic circuitry is hidden inside, and you can expose it by removing the upper chassis cover:

Our goal is to get these cars to run great (at least greater than in their stock form). To achieve this, you need to go through these steps and turn it into a "real" RC car: **Clean** → **Check** → **Replace electronics** → **Reinforce/Upgrade parts** → **Run**

<u>Below shows a quick overview of the process:</u>

First we have to clean up the original internals and fit new ones in.

We retain the power switch of the car. We solder the ESC power switch wires to this switch directly. We also replace the stock servo saver since it doesn't work well at all.

Be careful about the replacement servo arm you choose. If it does not have a proper size, the car will have unexpected toe-in or toe-out. The linkages on these cars are not adjustable!

Unexpected toe-out:

Completed:

Toy grade RC cars are not as sturdy as their hobby grade counterparts. The parts (often plastic) are brittle due to aging, and that all joints are likely loose giving room for play everywhere. Parts availability is another key concern. Vintage or not the manufacturers simply don't have that many spare parts produced (and in many cases those manufacturers were out of business decades ago already).

You must clean the car first so that any physical damage can become visible. Designs from the 80s and 90s are often unique and creative but less than solid. You need to carefully check everything exterior to find out and fix cracks (and you need to clean and remove the old crease and re-lube everything that spins). Mechanically, there are some parts that are constantly under stress (such as the arms, the turn knuckle and the front bumper) so you must make sure spare parts are available.

To be honest, like it or not you must be able to operate a very basic 3d printer. You will find it difficult to have replacement parts without doing some 3d printing on your own! The Proline RC Cyclone shown below has a 3d printed replacement front bumper and right turn knuckle.

Unlike hobby grade RC cars, toy grade RC cars do not use separate receiver and speed controller. They mostly use some sort of integrated circuitry (they call it PCB printed circuit board) for everything, which is easy to break and difficult to troubleshoot. PCB is cheap and easy to install, at the expense of performance and reliability.

This photo shows the PCB of a standard Jet Fighter.

Another thing very bad about these circuit boards is that they need separate power sources, which means extra weight being added to the car to slow it down.

The above photo shows the battery compartment of a Jet Fighter Twin Turbo. Some cells are wired to support only the electronic circuit and not the motor.

We always emphasize the need for replacing the electronics. You deserve more reliable radio and speed control! You may, for example, wanna use wheel/trigger based control instead of the toy-like sticks. Or you may need a more sophisticated transmitter that gives more adjustment options.

A real RC transmitter offers way more tuning options:

You may also want to have electronics that won't burn out as a result of much stronger battery power (lipo is the way to go but it produces output too strong for it). Let's face it, you will need a real ESC to do the job. Besides, with a real ESC you will not need to have separate power source for the receiver, allowing you to reduce the weight of the car and improve performance significantly.

You will likely need to make changes to the battery compartment as well. Lipo packs come in different sizes and with different connectors, which may not fit into your existing configuration. Many toy grade cars (including the Taiyo cars) simply use 8 x AA cells, while a few use the bulky Ni-Cd 7.2V (with plastic Tamiya plugs). All these will need to be upgraded accordingly to accommodate modern lipo power.

The suspension system may have to be upgraded too. Toy grade cars use spring based dampers that are too stiff to be practical. For better handling the dampers should be changed to something (oil based preferred) softer and more responsive. The photo below shows a Jet Fighter with its stock yellow damper replaced with a "better" one.

And you will want to reinforce weak structure (by using braces and other measures..). In any case you do not want to be too aggressive with your configuration. In fact, staying with the original motor would be your best bet for the sake of durability. This means the configuration would be a brushed one, as toy grade RCs never use brushless out of the box.

1/10 RC cars mostly use the Mabuchi RS540 stock motor. Smaller 1/12 cars use RS380 or RS370 instead. There are plenty of equivalent choices in the market so they can never be expensive.

BASIC TOOLS & SUPPLIES

When you need to make accurate measurement of anything, a precise gauge tool or caliper is always helpful. This is especially true when you need to make a replacement part on your own.

The size of a screw or bolt is normally specified as diameter, pitch and length, in millimeters ("mm"). In your RC manual you may see descriptions such as M1.6, M3 ...etc. M means Metric thread designation. To be simple, it is all about standard measurement of screw thread and sizes. You rely on this measurement to acquire the proper drive/wrench for dealing with the screws.

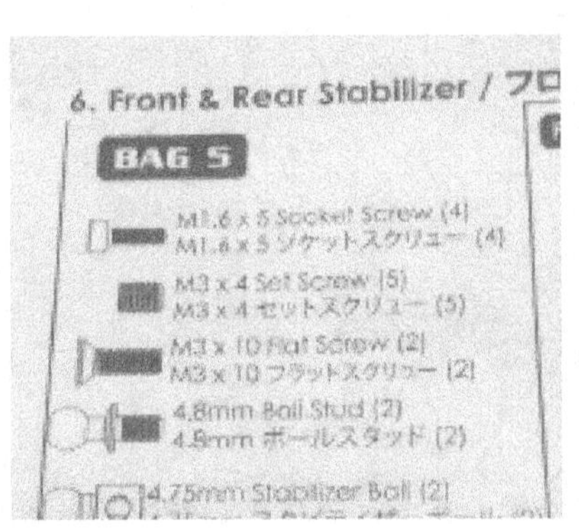

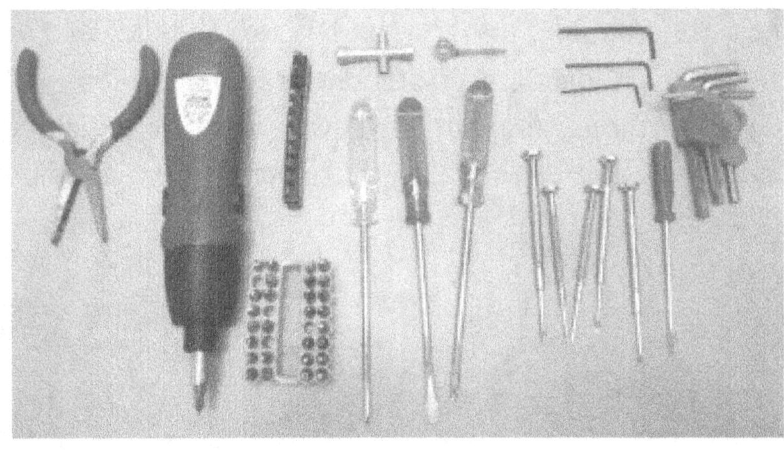

The two basic types of screwdrivers are standard (slot/flat head) screwdrivers and Philips screwdrivers. You should have both handy. Occasionally you will come across the need to work on smaller screws. Having a set of small drivers would definitely be beneficial. Using electric driver will definitely improve your productivity. For RC models, a simple 3.6V electric driver will do the job.

You will less likely need to use Allen wrench or Hex driver on toy grade cars. Keep in mind, large motor's pinion gear is always affixed via a tiny hex screw.

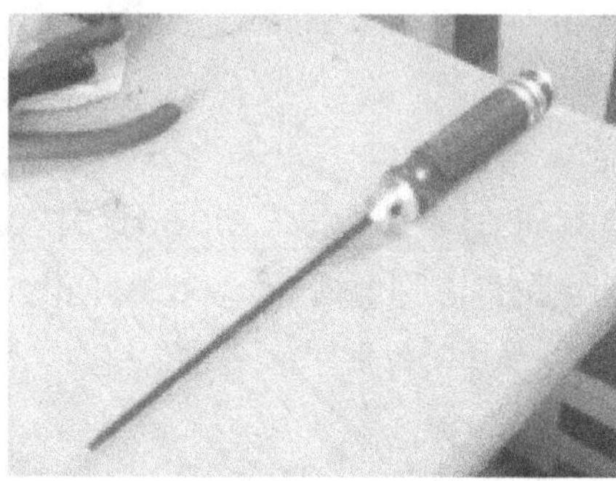

You may consider using screwholders for hanging onto screws that have to fit into tiny space. They have magnets to hold small metal parts. Some even have a little gizmo built-in for grabbing the screw.

Real RC cars often use linkage comprising ball caps and turnbuckle. As a coupling with internal screw threads for connecting two rods, a turnbuckle has its one end with a left-hand thread and another with a right-hand thread. Toy grade cars seldom use these because they don't expect things to be adjustable. You may, however, want to consider replacing the stock fixed length rods with these so that room for adjustment can be made possible.

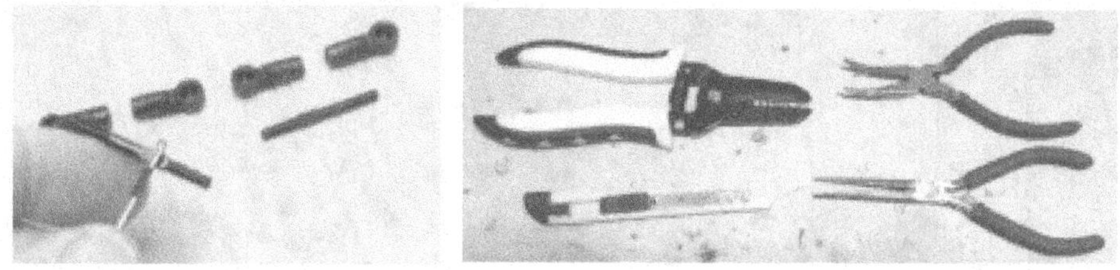

Hex nuts are common for securing the wheels and you will find hex nut wrench very useful.

You shall need needle-nosed pliers when handling smaller screws and nuts.

Combination slip-joint pliers are usually needed for handling relatively larger screws and nuts, even though they can be adjusted to several widths with a sliding pin. You may use razor knife for task that needs a very sharp edge, such as trimming plastic and decals. If you are new to electronics or basics of wiring, don't use razor knife to stripe wires as you will likely cut into the wire strands and thus lower the total overall diameter and size of the wire, which is generally a bad thing. The best thing to do is to use a wire stripper that has two cutting edges for cutting just the insulation of a wire and not the strands.

You may use a "E" Ring Clip Tool to effortlessly remove or insert "E" Rings (aka E clips). To be honest with you, I hate E clips! They are small and can become almost invisible once dropped on the floor.

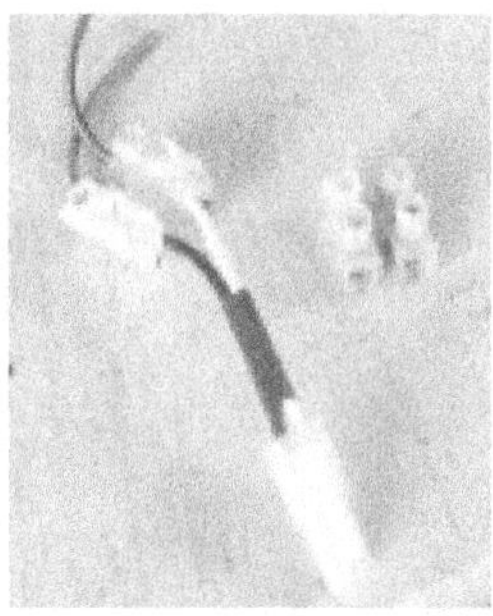

You need a pen shape soldering iron for replacing the stock circutry with real RC electronics, and you will likely need to perform rewiring of the power connection. If this is not what you want to get your hands on, make some of this wire connector ready (they can be bought from your local hardware stores).

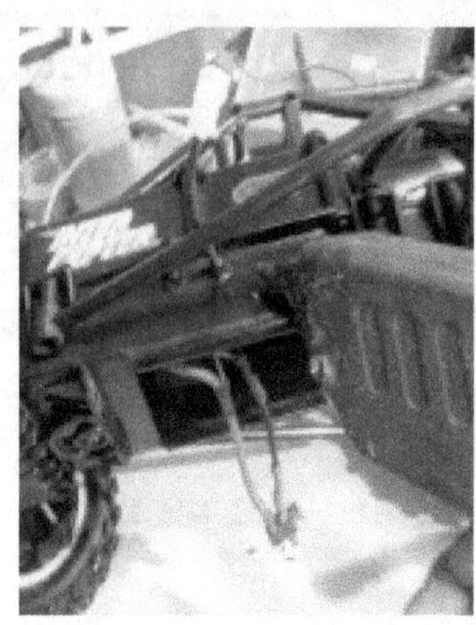 

A drill motor (and drill bit assortment) is necessary when you need to drill holes for wires to pass through or for mounting special add-on parts. You want one with variable speed control as a slow setting is needed when working with ABS plastic. Most of the time a hand operated drill is good enough as you should seldom need to do heavy duty drill works on your RC car.

You will need to use zip ties of different length. Lots of them. They are your best friend when something is broken and you need a quick fix. You will also need to use hot glue a lot. They can fix and secure things easy and quick, and what is done through it is always reversible.

And it won't hurt to have epoxy and super glue handy. Sometimes they can be used for quick fix so you don't waste your trip to the track.

3D PRINTING

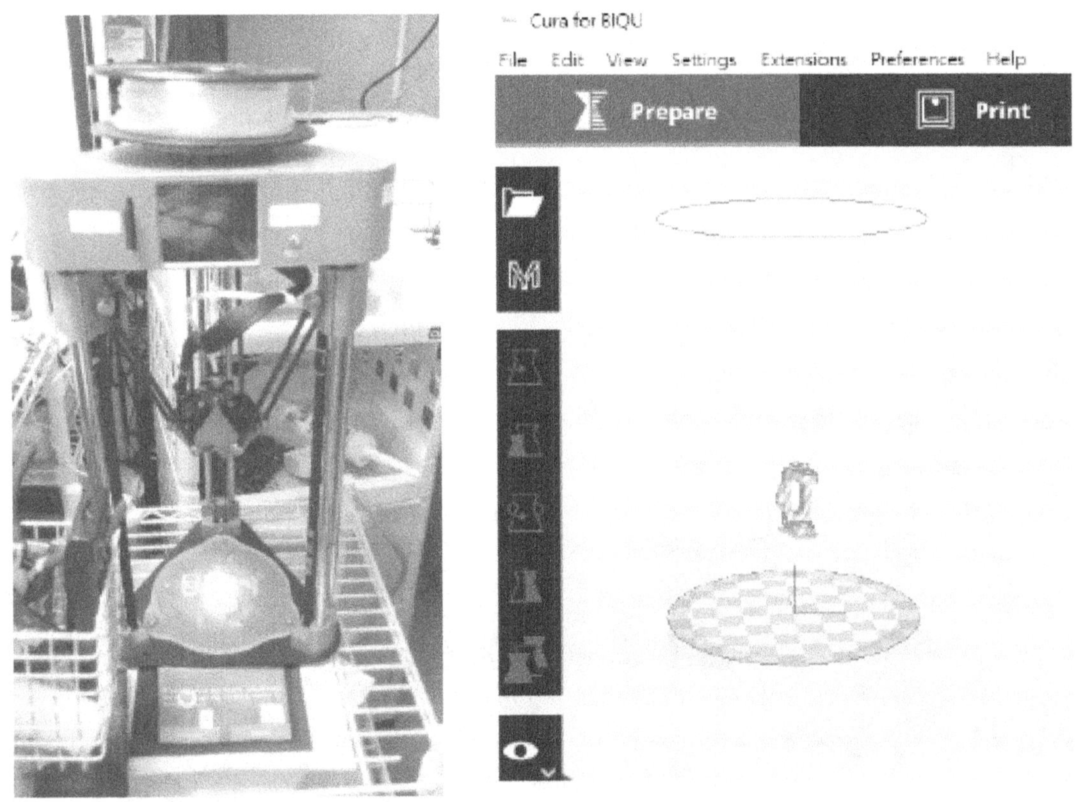

A 3D printer is a MUST! When there is a missing or broken part, chance is that the corresponding 3D file is already available on the web for free so you may simply download and print it out.

There are a lot of tech details regarding 3D printing which is out of the scope of this book, but you are strongly encouraged to explore further! For now you want to know that this is becoming more and more affordable so it wouldn't hurt to try it out.

When you 3D print parts for your RC car, there are a lot of followup works that must be done to ensure things can actually work as expected. Most of the time the parts you print are not 100% accurate in size and dimensions, and that the surfaces are usually rough. And unless you use 100% fill, the parts printed may still break on the track when under stress. The problem with 100% fill is that it uses more material and takes longer to finish the print. Still, I think it is worth it.

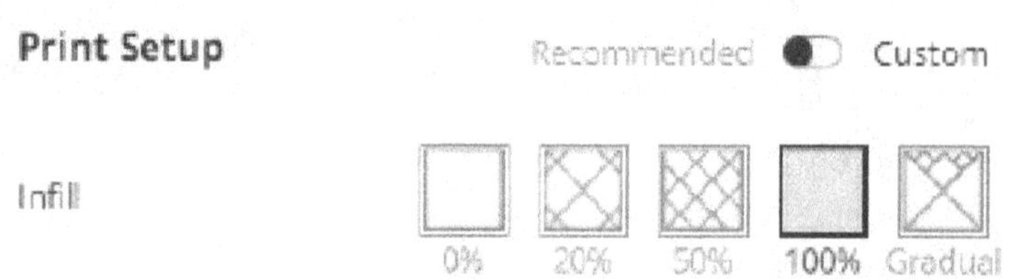

If you visit **upgradeparts.com** you will be able to find many free downloads for vintage cars.

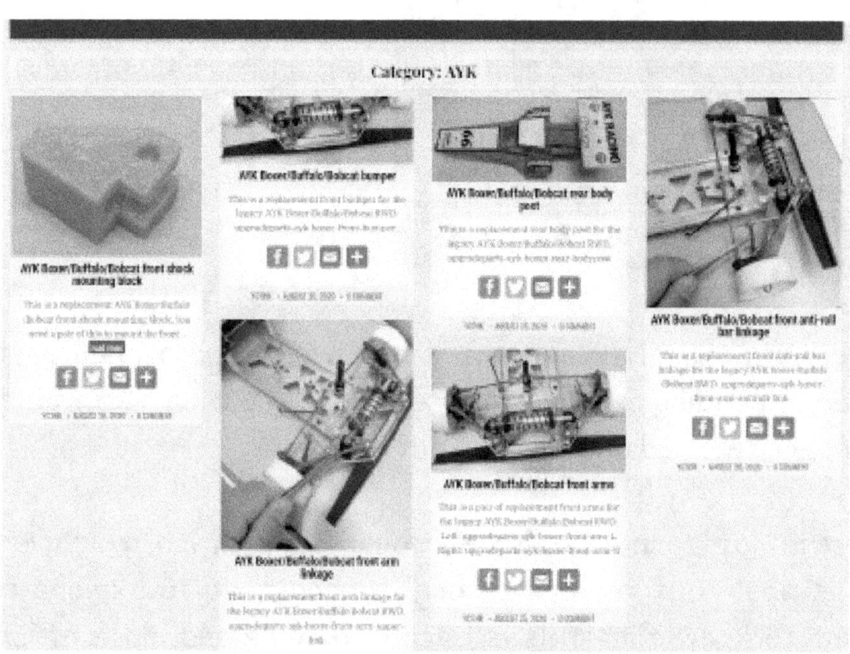

You may also design and 3d print fan mount for the motor and the ESC. I need to stress that many people ignore the importance of proper cooling. Unless you run your car in freezing Winter, get a cooling fan for the ESC and another for the motor. Even a brushed 540 motor would need proper cooling in summer.

the photo below shows a Bandai Intercepter that has a 3d printed fan mount at the rear end for cooling the motor. There is also a replacement rear lower arm:

This RC Proline Cyclone has a replacement 3d printed bumper and a front right turn knuckle.

Soldering Techniques

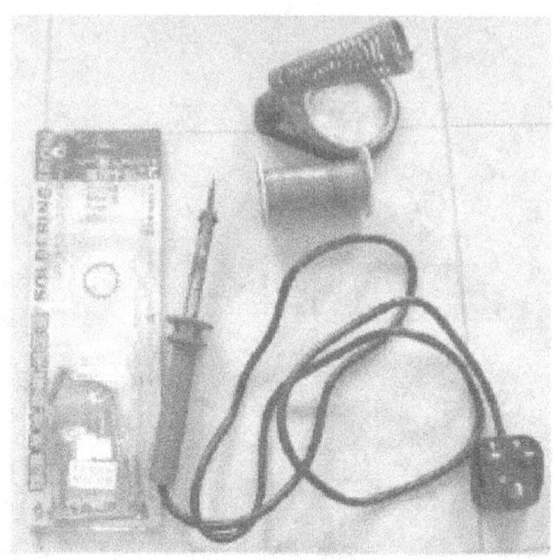

The goal of soldering is to join electrical parts together for forming an electrical connection. This is done via the use of a molten mixture of lead and tin (solder) with a soldering iron.

Basic supplies needed for proper soldering include a soldering iron (the prong of metal that heats to a specific temperature through electricity), the soldering wire (an alloy of aluminum and lead), and a cleaning resin called flux that ensures the joining pieces are incredibly clean (by removing all the oxides on the surface of the metal that would interfere with the molecular bonding, allowing the solder to flow into the joint smoothly). For hobby grade usage a 4mm 60-watt soldering iron is recommended. A 20-watt one would be too weak, while a 100-watt would be way too over-powered.

The first step in soldering is cleaning the surfaces (including the iron tip itself). They must all be clean and free from contamination. Then, you may melt flux onto the parts to be joined. The parts should both be heated above the melting point of the solder but below their own melting point with the soldering iron. When touched to the joint, this precise heating can cause the solder to flow and form a chemical bond. A perfectly soldered joint should be nice and shiny looking, and should be very reliable in service.

Soldering directly to the battery cells is never a good idea. You should only solder to the welded tabs. Soldering to the cell button can destroy the nylon seal. You simply can't get the cell button hot enough to get a good solder joint without compromising the integrity of the nylon seal ring.

Soldering of Lipo cells is dangerous and should never be done without professional help.

You will mostly need to do soldering when preparing connections for the cooling fan or changing the plug from Tamiya to deans. The Tamiya plugs are likely aged and no good anymore! Changing to deans is recommended. And make sure you have wire tube of different sizes handy. The soldered connections must be isolated and protected at all times.

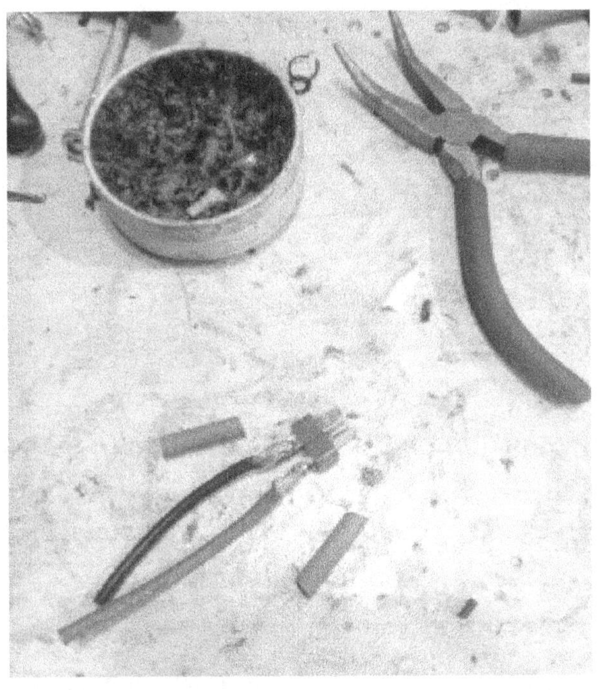

PROPER HANDLING OF THE SCREWS AND THE PLASTIC

Most amateurs tend to screw things very tightly in hopes that the parts will not fly off later. This is in fact a deadly mistake because some screws, bolts and nuts are NOT supposed to be tightened too securely or the threads would be stripped. If you find yourself confronted with a screw that is extremely difficult to get unscrewed, don't use brute force (or you risk stripping the threads). Instead, give the screw a slight twist in the opposite direction and then loose it again. If this does not help, tap the screwdriver on the head with a small hammer (but don't tap it too hard). If it still fails to make it, try to squirt the screw with penetrating oil or WD-40 and retry.

Use WD-40/RP7 with caution. WD-40/RP7 has a corrosive nature and is generally not recommended for use on plastic parts. To be safe, consider using silicon oil spray instead.

Stripping screws can be frustrating. If unfortunately you strip a screw, try to fill the stripped screw hole with J.B. Weld (which is a type of glue specially for use with metal parts), and then put your screwdriver into the old hole to create a new fitting. Give it 10 to15 minutes to set and dry completely, then unscrew it. If this doesn't work, simply drill a hole in the screw and scoop it out.

On the other hand, to prevent certain critical screws from getting loose, apply threadlock/locktite - a glue compound that makes screws more secure. Loctite usually won't bite into plastic very well. It can sometimes soften the plastic, but most of the time it won't really be permanently stuck on there. Most of the time you can get a locked screw loose via the use of a decent screwdriver (by the way, heat is what is used to release excessively strong locktite).

Generally speaking, there is no need to use locktite on a brand new RC car unless the car is going to run entirely on bumpy tracks (meaning the car is going to shake excessively all the time). Frequent disassembly can also make things loose. Therefore, locktite should be considered on critical parts like the nut that holds the wheel in place.

For vintage toy grade cars, the chance for screws to get loose is high. This is due to the fact that the screws are directly driven into the plastic body on most vintage designs. It is the plastic that holds the screw that is unreliable. Just like wood work where you drive screw directly into it, eventually it will wobble. Locktite would not help once the plastic is "bad". A quick and dirty trick is to cut and insert a small piece of toothpick into the screw hole. Or, wrap around the screw thread with water seal tape (this is ok only if the play is minimal).

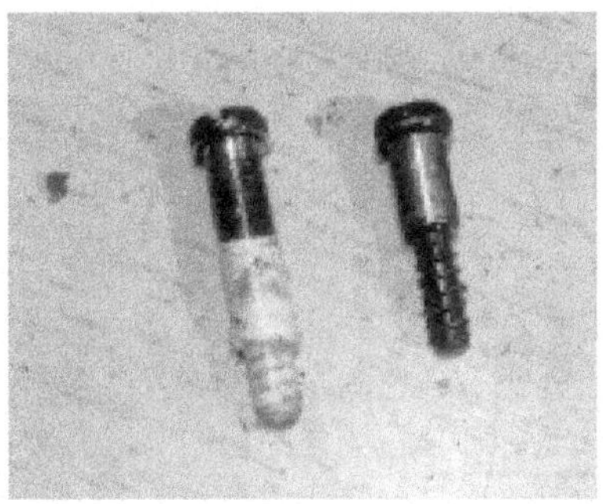

FYI, you can also instantly fix a hole or crack on the plastic chassis via the use of ramen and super glue. Easy and cheap! This method would not work on metal parts though.

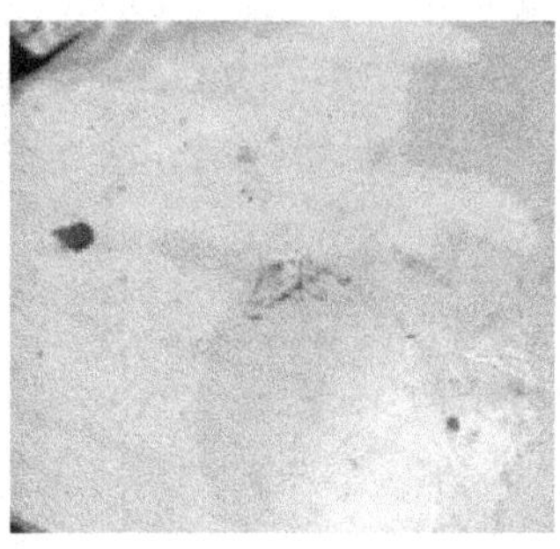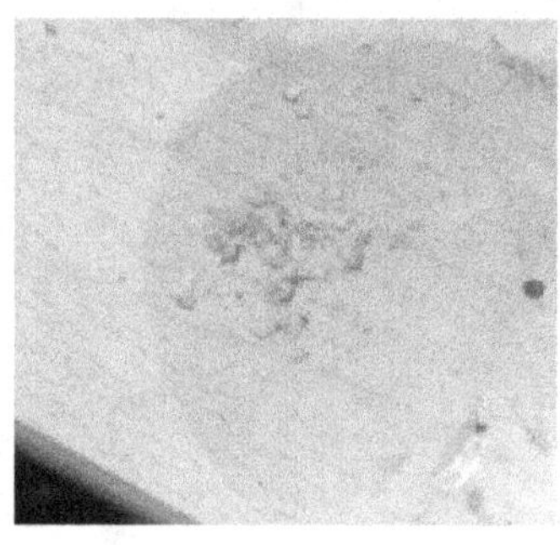

To avoid getting into chaotic situation when doing your assembly and disassembly works, try to be as organized as possible. Do your work on a clean, dry and flat surface which is close enough to reach without having to walk back and forth for grabbing the necessary tools. *In fact, it is best to work things out on a big white towel. The towel provides a color contrast, thus making it easy to see the parts as you lay them down.*

As you remove each part, lay it down on a clean flat surface in clockwise order, with each part pointing in the direction it laid when it was in place. Assign each part a number indicating the order in which it was removed. When you are ready to put them back together, start with the last part you removed and then go counterclockwise through the rest of the parts.

You may want to take photos of the car prior to disassembly. This is because toy grade car manuals are hard to find. Free downloads are likely unavailable.

INSPECTING A TOY GRADE RC CAR

With a used Toy Grade RC car, everything is in place so the first thing you would want to do is to check and ensure there is no severe physical damage on the chassis and the arms. Plastic (ABS) bodies are very popular among toy grade cars due to cost reasons. They are mostly made as kind of a bathtub for better protection against water and dust.

Small cracks like what is seen on the photo below are not structural and should not hurt:

Since you are going to replace the radios and the battery anyway, there is no need to check the electronics. The motor is a consumable item that can be easily replaced too.

Then check the differentials. There are 2 major types of RC differential gear. The gear based differential (gear diff) requires almost no tuning. Ball based differential (ball diff) gives more room for tuning (in fact it requires regular tuning and maintenance) but is said to be more troublesome (again, due to the need for careful tuning). Toy grade cars use gear diff only.

Why should we allow the wheels to rotate at different speeds? This is because the wheels actually spin at different speeds when turning. In fact, each wheel travels a different distance through a turn, and the inside wheels travel a shorter distance than the outside wheels (thus rotating at a lower speed due to the shorter distance). If the car has no differential gear in place, the wheels will be locked together and spin at the same speed. This will make turning very difficult and awkward - for the car to turn, one tire has to slip.

When you spin one wheel, the other one should spin in an opposite direction. If spinning is not smooth, chance is that some gears may be broken inside the gearbox. Coming up with a 3d printed gearbox gear is not always easy! You may have to draw one on your own, which may require rounds and rounds of trials (and errors).

A 3d printed middle gear:

Gear breakage can happen if you run your car on grassland and the grass is too long (so the entire drive system has to work very hard, putting all the stress on the middle gear). It can also happen if your motor is too fast for the aged gear.

Think twice before investing your time in upgrading and converting a toy grade RC car if the gears are bad. It is particularly difficult to create and print differential gears.

The coming photo shows a Nikko Black Fox rear drive system with broken gears inside. It is very difficult to just open up the gearbox since the wheels are VERY DIFFICULT top detach!

Stock toy grade cars usually come with a relatively small pinion, such as a 19T. Stick with what you have. Changing to a 23T can improve speed but may risk breaking the gears!

In its simplest form, the term "gear ratio" defines the relationship between the pinion gear and the spur gear. It addresses the concern of how many times the pinion gear has to rotate in order to make the spur gear turn around once. The "gearing" process actually reduces speed, not increases it. Such a speed reduction is necessary as it adds torque. Simply put, on the same motor less torque means:

1, higher top speed.
2, more stress imposed on the motor and the battery when going uphill.
3, more heat and higher energy consumption.

On the other hand, more torque means more power and better acceleration but less top speed. Anyway, toy grade RC cars are not too flexible in this regard. In fact they often come with a special motor mount design which limits the pinion you can use.

Another trouble maker is the tire. A bad rubber tire is almost impossible to repair. You can replace it with tires for real RC cars, but since they have different attachment mechanisms, you may need to come up with your own 3d printed wheel adapter. Real RC car wheels almost always use hex adapters, which may not be common on 1:12 or smaller toy grade cars.

    Copyright 2021. **The R.C.PRESS (Hong Kong)**. All rights reserved.

BEARINGS AND BUSHINGS

Bearings can reduce friction and facilitate smoother spinning by providing smooth metal rollers and a smooth inner and outer metal surface for the rollers to roll against. These rollers bear the load and allow the device to spin smoothly.

Toy grade RC cars may not come with bearings but plastic bushings. For used cars, it is always a good idea to clean the bushings using contact cleaner.

Changing from bushings to ball bearings will not deliver significant performance improvement but will make the drive system more reliable. Plastic bushings may break easily if you use a high speed motor. For regular toy grade RC motors the risk of bushing damage is low.

Bearings are structurally stronger and way more durable. If you come across spare bearings that are compatible with your toy grade car, it would not hurt to use them in place of the plastic bushings.

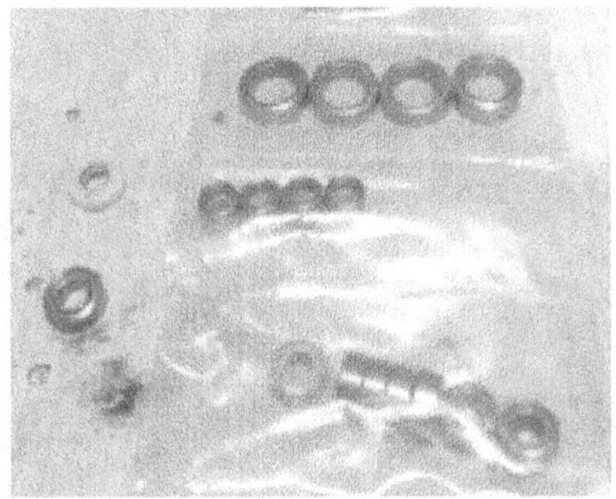

Ball bearings are often found in upgraded RC cars. They use small metal balls as the rollers. As long as you do not open up the gearbox you would likely not have any chance to fit ball bearings into the Taiyo cars.

DOG BONE SHAFT

You know what these shafts are for. When you change the stock suspension settings (dampers, mounting point ...etc) you may need to check and ensure the dog bones are stilling doing good when spinning. At each end (or on at least one end) of the dog bone there has to be room for "float" and flexibility.

There is no dog bone on any of the Taiyo 2WD frame buggies. Buggy such as the Jet Hopper and the Jet Fighter have a drive system at the rear end without independent suspensions and shafts.

Motors and Cooling

Most off-the-shelf Toy Grade RC cars are shipped with the Mabuchi RS series motors. The 540 motor is for 1:10, while the 380/370 are for 1:12 or smaller cars such as the Taiyos. They are all closed endbell motors with two wires. You are free to reverse the motor connections without breaking anything (it affects the direction of spinning and nothing else).

Aged motor requires conditioning and cleaning. You cannot replace the brushes on these closed end bell motors. But you can use contact cleaner to flush clean the inside of the motor, which is usually good enough to restore performance.

Heat will weaken the magnets of the motor. It is not uncommon for motors to get overheated and stop working. This is why in our demo units a special cooling fan is added to the configuration.

The fan is a small 5V DC fan 20mm in size. First a 3d print fan mount is attached to the frame using hot glue. Then you secure the fan onto the mount, again with hot glue (and screw if there is screw hole available).

The fan has a small connector, allowing easy fan replacement in case the fan goes bad. You want to draw power from the main battery connection. There is a rationale behind this and we will talk about this later. For now you want to know that soldering is required.

If you want connectors that can sustain high current, Deans connectors is the way to go. Modern lipo packs can produce current too strong for the Tamiya connectors to last even though they are physically small and light-weight.

With Deans connectors, the Female side is connected to the battery pack. Deans not only produce less resistant, but are physically more reliable too.

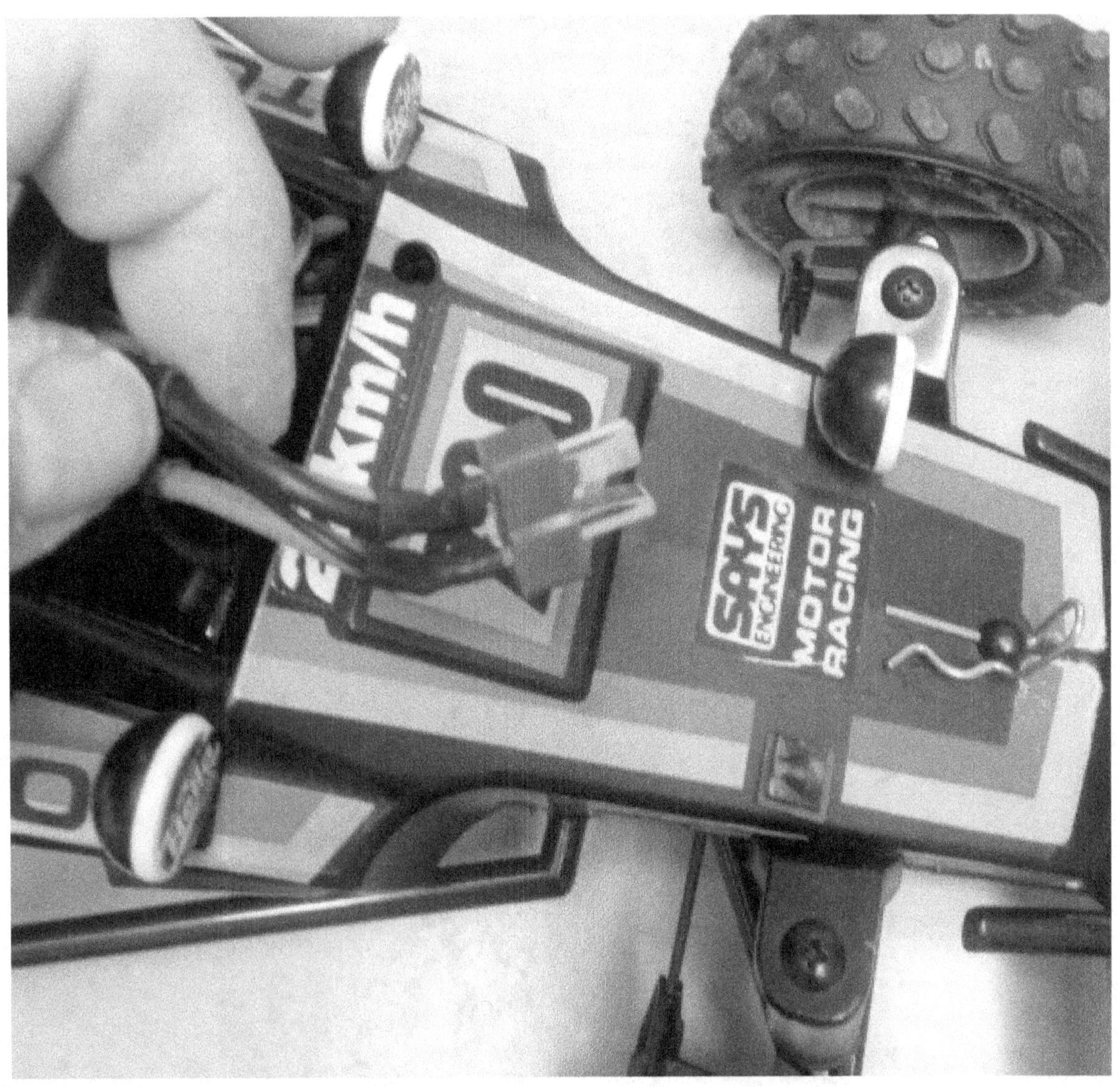

You need to make a small hole on the side of the battery compartment so the thin fan wires can reach the outside to the fan. Remember to wrap the wires with wire tube for protection.

FYI: There are many 3d print mounts available on upgradeparts.com:

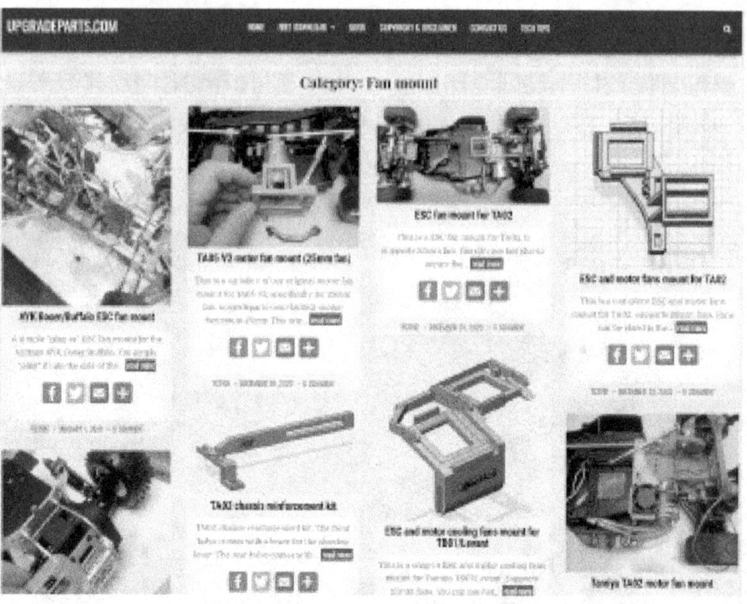

Smaller frame buggies use AA cells for everything. One bad thing about AA cells is that the electrical contacts can get oxidized pretty easily. Therefore we recommend that you dispose the AA cell mechanism entirely and change to 2S lipo pack. We will show you how later.

5V or 12V DC fans are fine (you don't need 12V power to push a 12V DC fan since the fan will still spin slower with a lower input voltage, and all you need is to cut the yellow wire). If you use a 5V fan you may get power from the ESC-to-receiver connection (through the red and black wires, after you replace the circuitry of your toy grade car with real RC stuff) or from a separate source. Since most 5V fans can work under higher voltage, seeking power from the main battery is the most straight forward option.

I would strongly recommend that you avoid drawing fan power from any source other than the battery. when you get power from the battery directly, the fan is always on as soon as the battery is connected. Using JST connectors for this purpose would be the most convenient (fan replacement made easy should it fail), although XH2.54 will also be fine.

The tricky thing about small DC fan is that you must get the POS and NEG right. Therefore make sure red goes to red and black goes to black. A bit of clarification here: RED is always POS and BLACK is always NEG. Sometimes WHITE may be used in place of BLACK but RED is always RED. On another note, we found that some Taiyo/Nikko RC cars use brown wire for POS and blue wire for NEG...

When you cannot afford to have a cooling fan, a motor heatsink can help a bit. The thing is, a heatsink may not fit in given the mounting position of the motor. When there is no room for the heatsink, you will have no choice but a fan.

The photo below shows a RC Proline Cyclone RWD with a RS380 motor and a heatsink.

On the other hand, this Nikko Blackfox has the motor almost completely enclosed so there is no way you can put a heatsink onto it.

The Taiyo cars have heat sink built in already, this is why attaching a fan to it is not difficult at all.

Modifying Suspension

The job of the suspension system is to maximize the friction between the tires and the road surface and to provide steering stability with good handling, which in turn allows for a smoothly controlled ride. Generally speaking, the four wheels work together in two separate systems, which are the two wheels connected by the front axle and the two wheels connected by the rear axle. A dependent system has a simpler structure but is less effective for shock absorption and traction control. In fact, dependent rear suspensions have not been used in mainstream RC cars for years. But on these vintage Taiyo cars, the rear end is always a dependent system.

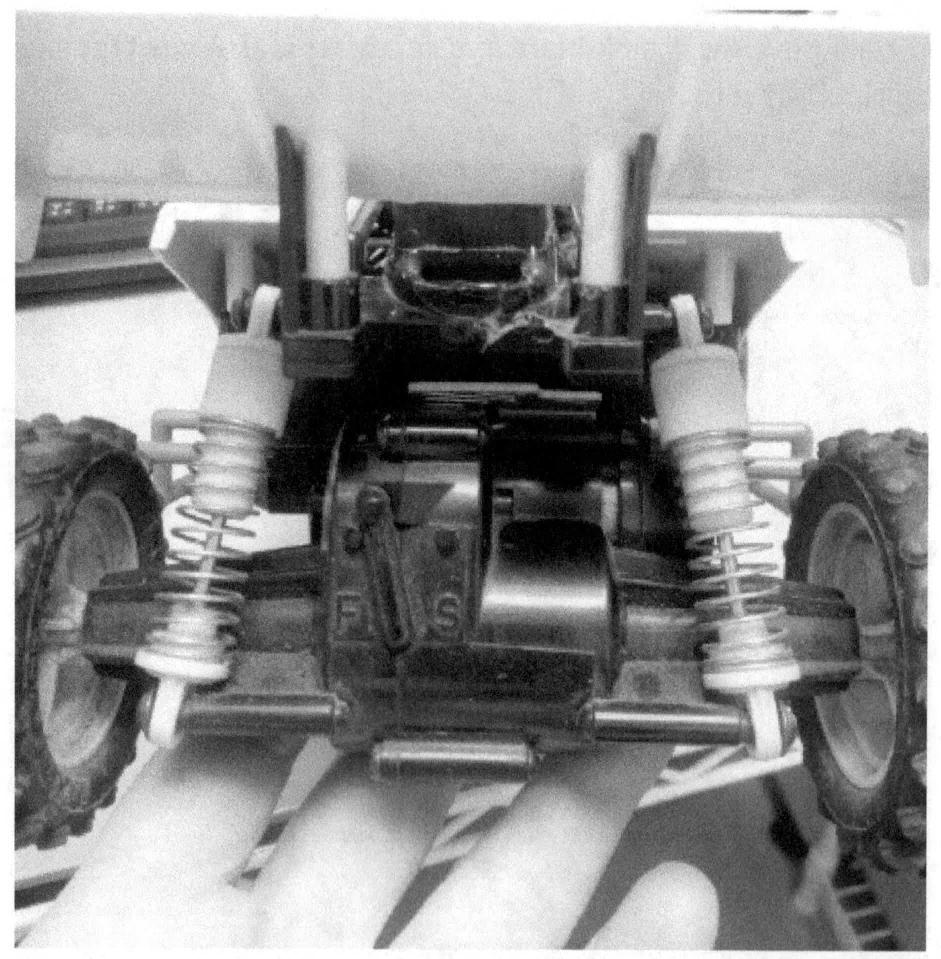

The primary components of a suspension system are dampers. A damper acts as a shock absorber. It is basically a tube like device placed between the chassis of the car and the wheels. The upper mount of the damper connects to the frame, while the lower mount connects to the axle near the wheel. The 2 major types of RC damper are oil filled shock absorber and pure spring based damper. Toy grade RC cars exclusively use the latter, while higher end real RC cars always use the former. Don't be fooled by their look. They copy the look of the popular Tamiya plastic dampers but they are never oil based.

We found that almost all toy grade cars come with spring based dampers that are way too stiff to be useful. For many cars, the stock dampers have to be replaced with true oil dampers in order to be "compress-able". An true oil filled shock absorber allows for smoother response to differing road conditions through slowing down (smoothing out) the movement of the spring (the "smoothing out" effect can be fine tuned through using different grades of damper oil, which is commonly described by thickness but measured in weight – 10wt is the thinnest while 100wt is the thickest). The thicker the oil the "harder" the damper is. Keep in mind, those with "softer" suspension can swallow bumps for smoother ride but is prone to dive and squat during braking and acceleration and may easily roll while cornering. Those with "harder" suspension are less capable of swallowing bumps on bumpy roads but can minimize body motion better, which is more suitable for an aggressive driving style.

The above picture shows the inside of a true oil damper. It is not unusual for the piston rod to get oily after a ride or two. Make sure you keep it clean all the time as dirt often likes to stick to the oily surface. Also check the oil level of your shock absorber regularly. Insufficient oil inside the absorber can lead to slower rebound. Refill if necessary. AND make sure you put in the same amount of oil for the left and right absorbers! Also, immediately check the suspension system after each crash. The piston rod may be bent during a crash. For information on how to choose shock oil and fill up the absorber properly, please use this app (which is free from our web site):

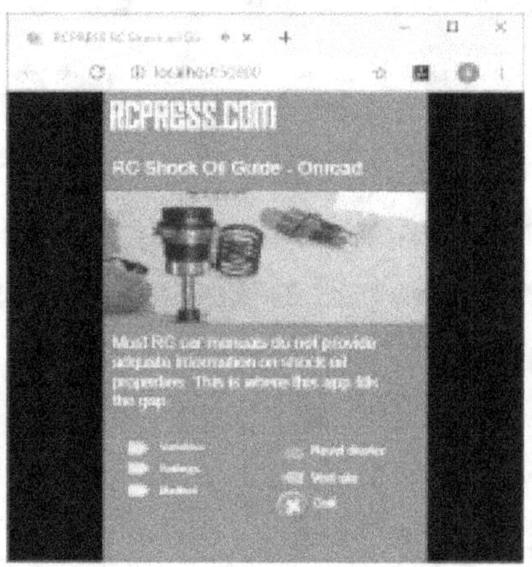

A common problem with aged shock is oil leak, not due to breakage but a loose shaft assembly. It may be a good idea for you to remove the shock absorber and take it apart so to assess the extent of leakage, damage and wear (if any). Drain the remaining oil, clean everything and refill with new oil. If the piston rod is bent, you will need to replace it (or replace the entire damper if replacement piston rod is hard to find).

When refilling, always do this from the top. The priority is to ensure no air bubble remains. You will need to move the piston up and down SLOWLY and let them sit still for a minute until all the air bubbles in the oil is gone. The pictures below shows the filling of a plastic Tamiya oil damper.

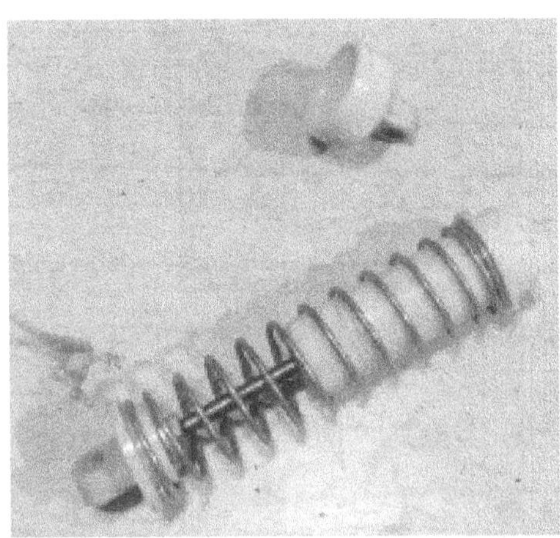 

The angle of the damper can also make a difference. Some real RC car models allow you to fine tune the mounting angle of the dampers independently, while others may require that you drill holes on your own (or 3d print a special mount) to change the mounting positions. In any case, horizontal mounting (like what we have on the Jet Fighter) is never effective (give it a try - you have to press real hard for the suspension to suspend). In fact most of the time it is the grass (and the tires) that absorb the "shock". Therefore you should use real oil dampers with a softer setting so they can actually catch and absorb the shock on behalf of the chassis.

Different dampers may have mounting holes of different sizes. Real RC uses ball stud a lot for mounting dampers. If you don't have them, step screws or regular screws wrapped with hottube/wire tube can serve similar purpose.

Ball stud: 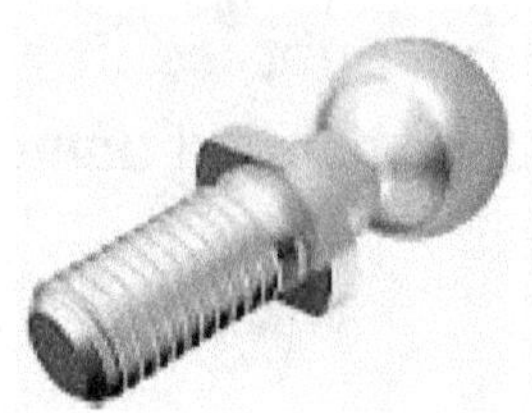   Step screws: 

The stiffness of your suspension system determines the ride height. **A low ride height tends to give better stability and is generally good for onroad racing only.**

It is perfectly fine if you intentionally make either the front or the rear stiffer. In fact, a stiffer rear suspension can lead to a higher ride height at the back, which allows for more steering. HOWEVER, it is NEVER okay for one side of the car to go stiffer than the other side (we are talking about left/right stiffness here). Left/right balance must ALWAYS be maintained.

One easy way to determine if your existing dampers are too soft for the track is to check the bottom of the chassis after each ride and see if new scratches are popping out all over the place. To determine if proper left/right balance is maintained, see if these scratches are evenly distributed.

FYI, a double wishbone suspension has both an upper arm and a lower arm on each side. Such an architecture is more solid and sturdy when comparing to a single wishbone design commonly used by smaller scale RC cars. The Jet Fighter has a double wishbone design at the front.

Since the arms are fixed in size and length, there is no way you can adjust the camber. To allow for camber adjustment you need to 3d print a shorter upper arm (for negative camber) or replace the upper arm with adjustable rod. For general enjoyment purpose I don't think this is necessary though. Camber refers to the vertical angle of the tire in relation to the ground. Camber adjustment aims at controlling how much tire and traction is grabbing the track surface at any moment.

The Taiyo Jet Hopper uses single wishbone at the front. No upper link at all!

The RC Proline Cyclone frame buggy also has a front single wishbone design. In fact, this design is pretty common among toy grade 2WD RC cars.

INSTALLING REAL RC ELECTRONICS

The circuitry inside the toy grade car should be disposed entirely. You need to free up space to accommodate the real stuff.

A basic overview of the real RC electronics will be helpful here. The most popular controller set for RC cars is the pistol grip 2-channel system. With a 2 channel system you can control steering with one channel (channel ONE) and throttling with another (channel TWO). A receiver is an electronic device that receives radio signal from the controller and decodes the signal for controlling the servos. Modern 2.4G transmitters are bundled with pre-bound receivers. It is possible to bind it to multiple models, each with their own setup and refinements saved as profiles. Traditional AM radio requires that you use matching crystals on both sides - the process is manual. In this example we use a pair of crystal @ 26.095hz:

If you want to retain the look of a vintage toy grade car, you need to retain an antenna. A simple wire inside the long plastic tube that stands firmly on the chassis is all that you need.

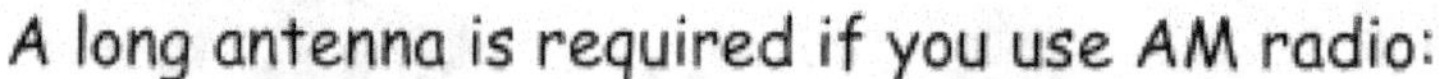

A long antenna is required if you use AM radio:

2.4G radio has shorter antenna: 

A very obvious advantage of deploying 2.4Ghz radio is that you no longer need a very long "antenna" on both sides. There are still antennas, but they are much shorter. If you use a traditional AM radio receiver, you must make room for establishing an antenna on the chassis. There are way more available channels (there are about 80 channels in the 2.4GHz band) for you to choose from. In fact, some higher end transmitters will automatically select and lock onto clear channels for you. The thing is, with 2.4G radio the receiver must match the transmitter - they better be from the same manufacturer!

Modern 2.4G transmitters often come with beautiful LED display for making configuration settings. Good for hi tech geeks (but may not be so for old guys who hate computer tech).

Of all the fancy features, fail safe mode is the most valuable – it will stop the car if the radio does not function. Definitely valuable for vintage runners too costly to crash!

Connecting a capacitor to the receiver can be useful if you suspect that there is radio interference somewhere within your system. There are ready made capacitors that can be connected directly to the receiver.

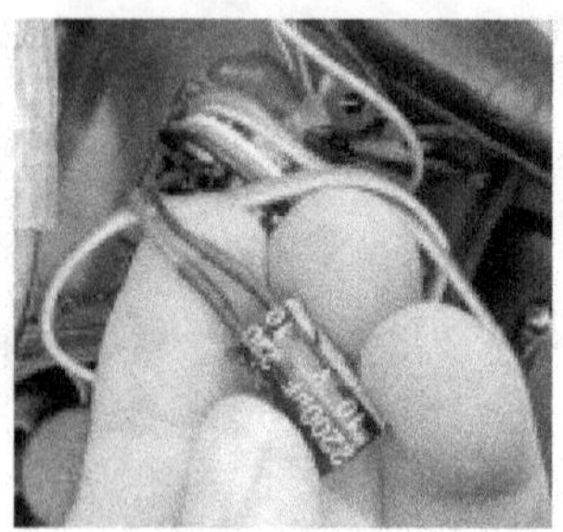

A servo (servomechanism) is a device for providing mechanical control remotely. RC servos use an electric motor for creating mechanical force (and giving rotary output). RC cars rely on servos for two purposes: for steering and for throttling (through controlling the mechanical speed controller).

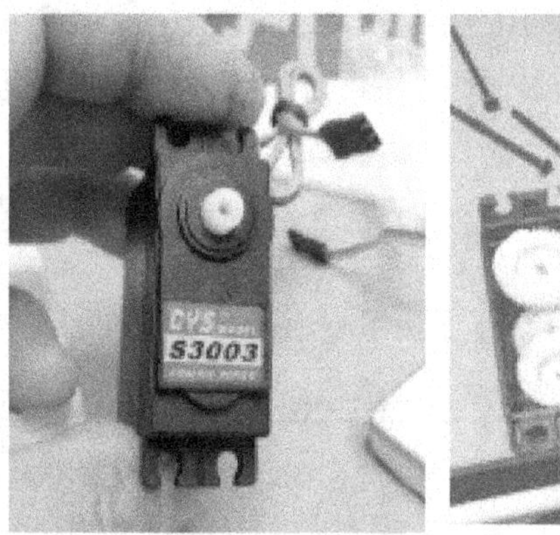 

Inside the servo you can find a number of gears. If any of these is broken, your servo is dead. A servo saver is a piece of white plastic device with a built-in spring for connecting the steering rods to the servo's output shaft. Its primary use is to absorb shock during driving or upon a crash. It is breakable, and in fact you want it to break upon a crash such that the servo itself can be free from any impact.

Modern transmitters provide many options for in-depth configuration. Some of the more common options are described here. Steering Dual Rate gives you the ability to control the amount of travel on either or both directions on the steering servo. Throttle dual rate can be used for throttle endpoint adjustment. If there is an End-point Adjustment function, you can have end points adjusted individually in percentage for left and right as well as forward and back. Exponential Adjustment is a highend feature that allows you to modify the behavior of transmitter inputs - think of it as behavioral response to your trigger action that "behaves" like a curve line in a graph.

Legacy RC radios are either AM or FM based. The crystal is either AM or FM specific and you can tell from the label attached to it. The crystals must match on both sides!

Not all Radio Control Systems share the same wiring scheme. Therefore, if you are mixing and matching components of different brands, find out the schemes they use so you can properly connect them together. For receiver and servo, you want to ensure the wire plug is compatible. Different brands have different wiring scheme for the plug, so compatibility is not always guaranteed. The almost universal standard is Futaba. Almost all receivers in the market can take Futaba connector plugs by default. The wires are white – red- black.

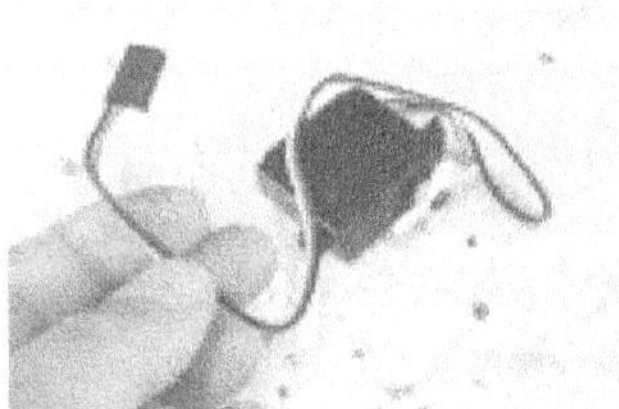

To connect receiver and ESC/servo produced by different manufacturers, you may need to do some work on the connector. Say, if the connector plug has a shape that cannot fit into the receiver port BUT the wires seem to match (based on their colors, for example – White, Red, Black), one dirty trick is to ply open the plastic shell of the receiver and file away the plastic that blocks the plug.

If the wire coloring is different, REMEMBER there is always one sure fire way to hurt the receiver – that is, by having the RED wire in the wrong place. ALMOST ALL coloring schemes include a RED wire, and that RED wire carries power. If you put that in the wrong contact pin your receiver will suffer.

Always test everything before putting them into your car. Especially with modern 2.4G devices, compatibility can become quite questionable. In particular you must ensure that you are using the correct receiver with the correct transmitter. Check the serial number label on both and make sure they match. If they don't, things won't work. If they do, then make sure the ESC goes to channel 2 of the receiver.

If you are using the legacy AM radio, always make sure you are using the proper pair of crystals. I have seen so many problems with bad quality crystals which stop things from working as expected…

When you arrange the electronics, make sure the receiver does not stay too close to the motor. The motor is the biggest source of radio interference.

When you attach the servo arm to the servo, make sure the arm has the right spline for proper mating. There are different servo arms for servos with different spline. There are 25-, 24- or 23- spline variations out there. Futaba is 25. For the servo arm to fit perfectly with the servo, the number of spline must match.

When you remove the circuitry from the car, you are effectively removing the receiving function (and may be the speed control function too). Now there is plenty of room for placing the real RC electronics.

On the Taiyo cars, the circuitry serves the purpose of a receiver and also a speed controller. We will talk about speed controller later. For now you can do a little bit of test fitting - try to put the real RC electronic stuff onto the empty deck and see how things look.

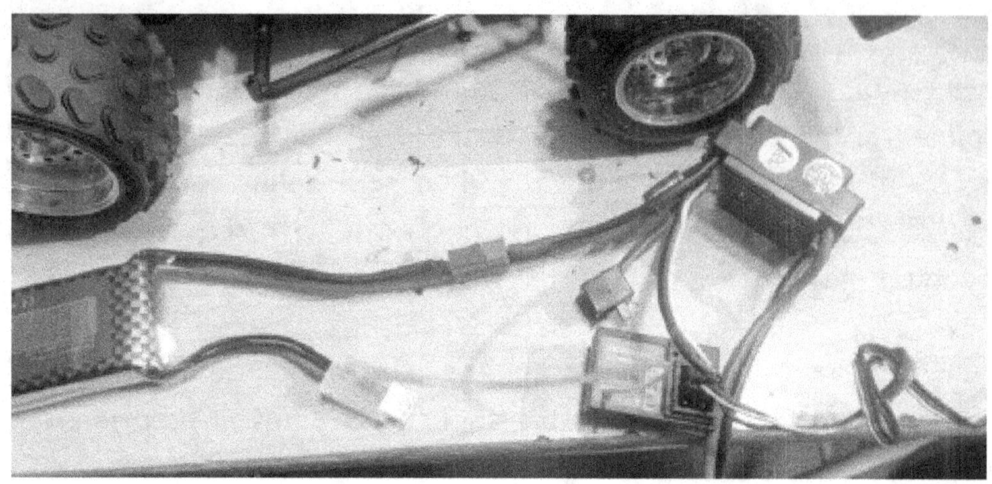

There is a decision you need to make right here. The circuitry was completely covered by a plastic block. Since a toy grade car was not expecting very high power, heat was never a concern. As we upgrade it to real RC, you need to be very careful in determining where to place the electronics, particularly the ESC as it can get very hot (due to hot weather and/or extreme workload brought by a high power Lipo pack).

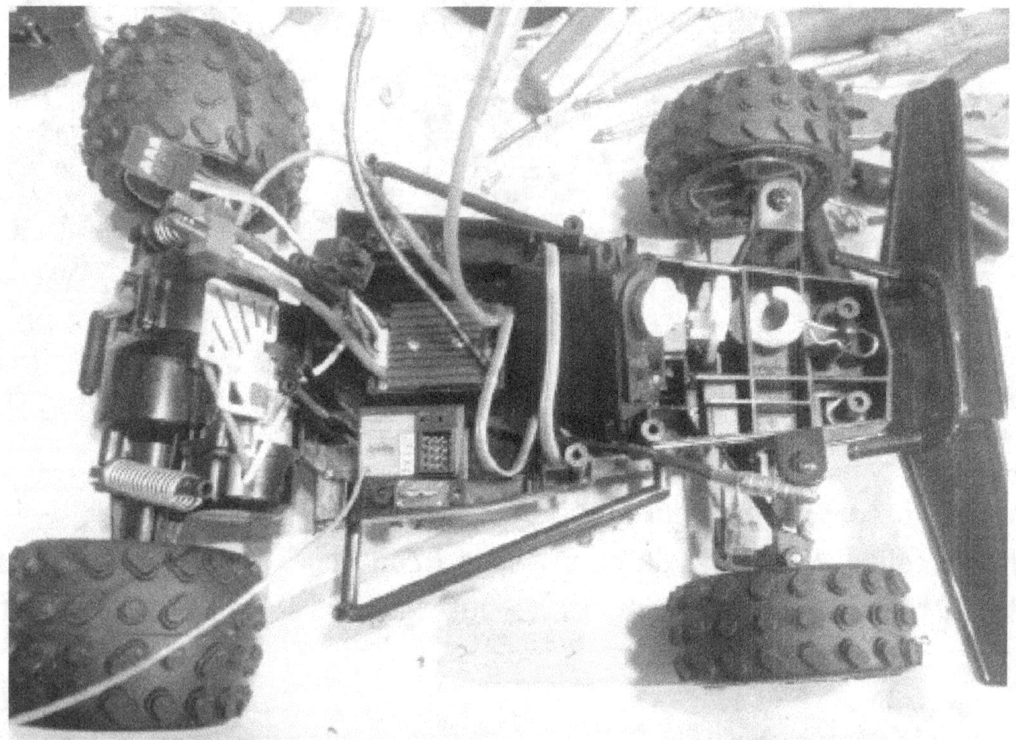

To be safe, you should always mount the ESC in a position where air can freely flow across it. That means you should not hide it inside a sealed frame. Thermal protection is available on many ESCs but you should not rely on this feature alone! This is a tradeoff - if you want to have proper cooling, you will need to remove anything that blocks the air flow. NEVER place the ESC inside a closed compartment!

When choosing a brushed ESC, makes sure you get one that supports at least 20A current in forward mode for the Taiyo cars. 30A would be even better. The connections to the motor should be properly soldered. OR, if you want the connections to be "portable", give the motor wires a bullet connector. Mixing up the POS and NEG of the motor wires won't hurt since it is just a matter of spinning direction (but mixing up the battery wires will kill the electronics instantly!).

Another thing - you will find that a servo is still there. This servo is functionally a servo but is not the same as the real RC servo. From the photo you can see that it has more than 3 wires (real RC servo has 3 wires, mostly following the color scheme of red, black and white), so it is not going to work with a real RC receiver.

1:10 real RC servos all share the same physical size and they should fit in easily. However, the problem is with the spline size of the servo saver. They are not always the same.

In our demo unit, the Futaba servo has a spline size too large to fit with what is provided by the Jet Fighter, so we choose another servo that has a smaller spline.

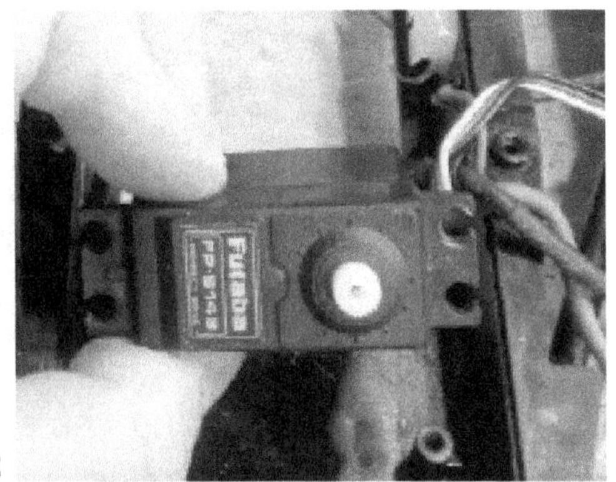

This is a standard real RC servo:

These two have different spline sizes:

Use double sided tape at the bottom and hot glue at the sides to secure the servo.

Before moving on, first hook up the electronics and test the servo. It is very important to center it (that is, you adjust the steering to the center position) right now. This will save you troubles when putting back together the steering mechanism.

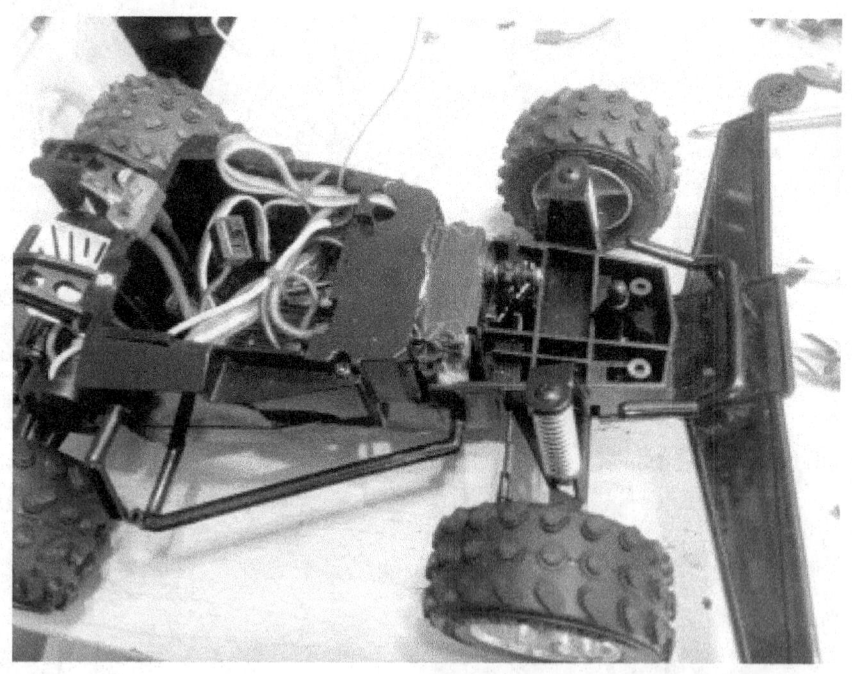

When the electronics are working, you can put everything into the proper location (I personally prefer to have them located in accessible locations for ease of maintenance). Secure them with double sided tape at the bottom and hot glue at the sides. Finally you can attach the servo saver to the servo , then reassemble the chassis and the front ends.

After putting everything together, use zip ties to organize the wires and make sure they don't get in the way of the cooling fan. The power switch of the new ESC can be hot glued to the side.

The switch should be in an accessible location:

Keep in mind, battery low on either side (the transmitter or the receiver) can lead to poor range or render your RC car inoperable. Always use good quality alkaline cells on the transmitter. Newer transmitter models allow you to use lipo pack, which is less troublesome than regular AA cells. If your car does not steer even when battery is not low on both sides, check whether the connection between the servo and the receiver remains intact. If the connection has not been terminated, try to use another servo to test and find out if this is a receiver problem or a servo problem.

If your car is going too fast and you do not know how to adjust the ESC, a quick fix is to set the transmitter's TH Trim value as well as the TH EPA H/L values. A lower value on these can reduce both the top speed and the acceleration, making the configuration safer for the gear.

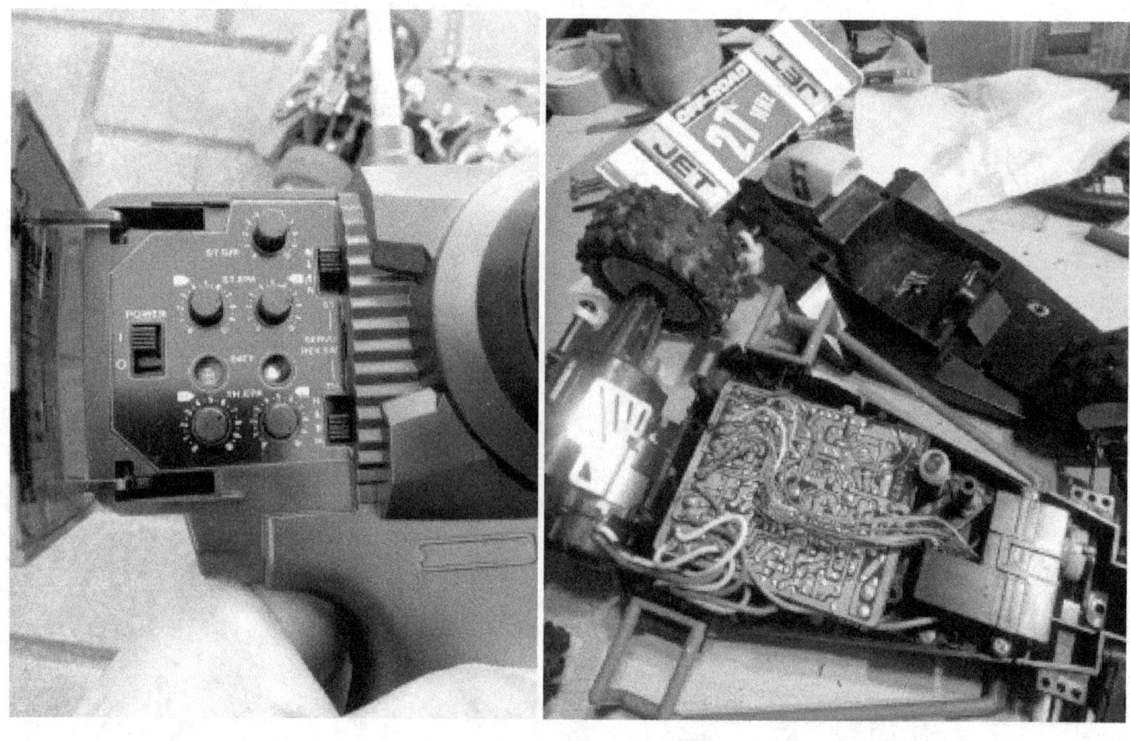

The Jet Fighter has a similar but not identical architecture. JetHopper has the battery compartment accessible from the top. The JetFighter has the compartment at the bottom. In any case you will need to get rid of the circuit board and the existing servo.

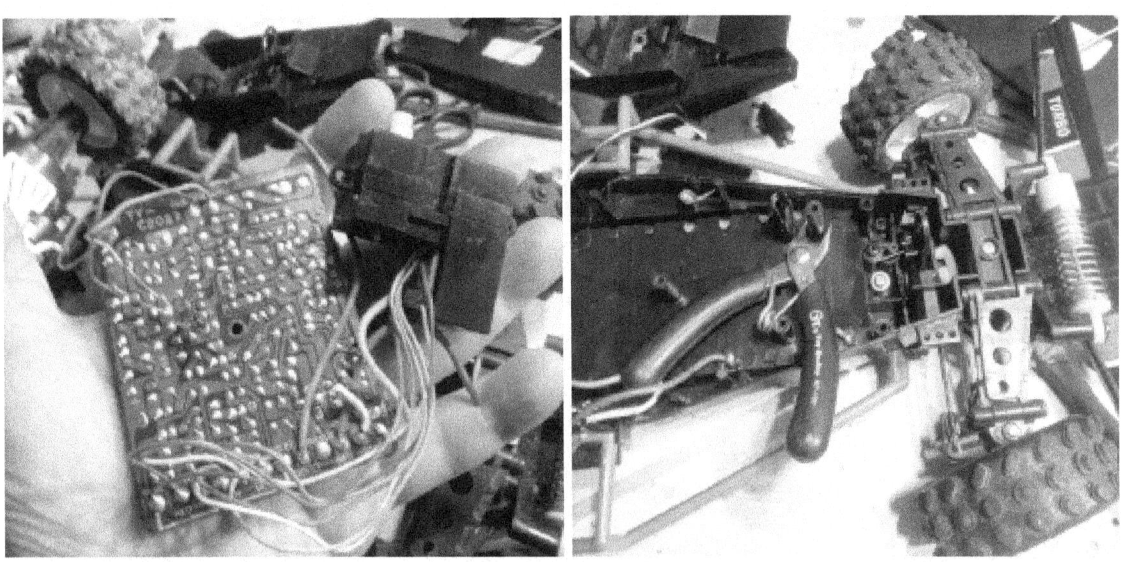

After removing the circuitry and the unnecessary plastic columns from the chassis, you will find plenty of room for accommodating a receiver and a servo. Do make sure your servo is compatible with the spline size of the servo saver.

If you use a standard size servo you need to cut away the plastic on the sides. You use double sided tape and hot glue to secure it (there are smaller servos in the market but they offer less torque). Make sure nothing blocks the servo from turning smoothly:

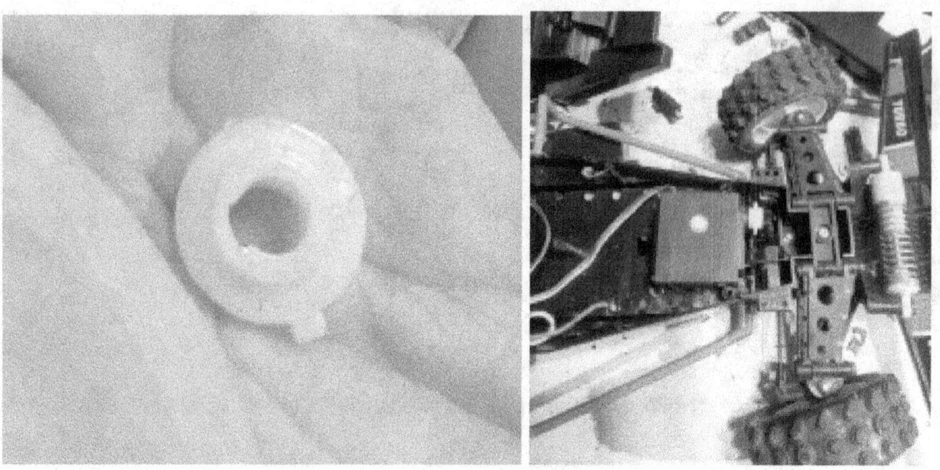

As a matter of fact, the servo savers that come with the toy grade cars are not too reliable. The C ring is not strong enough to sustain the power of the replacement servo. If your car cannot run a straight line (randomly), just get rid of the servo saver and use the part that comes with your servo. These cars are not fast so you do not really need to worry about a servo crash.

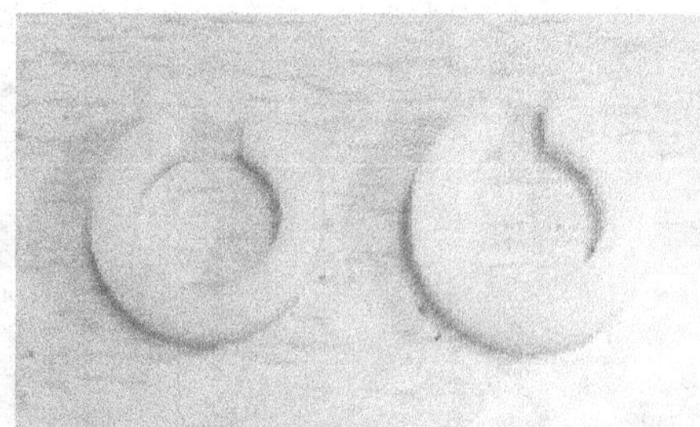

The stock C rings:

Replace the stock servo saver with this servo arm:

You may need to remove some plastic from the sides so the new steering mechanism can work smoothly. You can find out what to remove through some test steerings.

The stock servo saver has been replaced:

The motor has an existing small heatsink already:

Bullet connectors are soldered to the motor. Testing of the electronics is conducted to ensure things work fine.

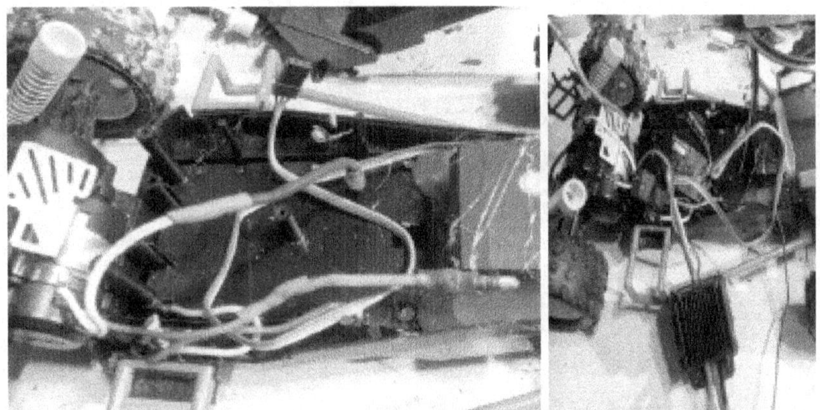

The Jet Fighter uses a 370 motor, which does not draw much current. You don't really need a very powerful ESC for it. One capable of 20A forward would be good enough (although using a stronger one will not hurt).

If you use AM receiver here, the receiver wire can be soldered to the existing antenna of the car. Or you can set up a separate antenna. Keep in mind, AM radio receiver is physically larger in size than the 2.4g counterpart! If you do not have much space here, go with a 2.4G radio!

The battery compartment is relatively small so a much smaller Lipo pack is to be expected. An extension wire is made available so that the ESC can stay at the top while the battery can stay in the bottom compartment.

The receiver does not generate any heat so it can stay inside the chassis. The ESC needs air circulation so it must stay on top of the chassis deck.

Completed:

BATTERIES

Lipo is the way to go. It is smaller, lighter and is way more powerful! A 7.2V 3700mah nimh pack is so strong that when it is fully charged its effective voltage output is very close to 8.88v. Size-wise, a very close alternative to 7.2V nimh is 7.4V Lipo. Lipo is less heavier and far more powerful. A good 7.4V lipo can easily achieve 9V+ when fully charged and it is safe for the ESC's BEC circuit!

The photo above shows lipo packs of different sizes. FYI, there are many free 3D files that can be downloaded from the web for making standardized battery case.

For smaller 1:12 toy grade cars you really need some smaller batteries. See this one, the Jetfighter original battery compartment has been cleaned up to have as much space as possible so a small 2S lipo can be squeezed in.

The Jethopper does not have a compartment at the bottom so we use a creative way to accommodate the battery.

The use of Lipo requires extra care. As a general rule, the proper storage voltage is max 3.8V per cell. Sitting fully charged for over a week can harm the battery! On the other hand, never discharge your Lipo battery below a certain minimum voltage (we refer to it as the cut-off voltage). We have an app that helps you look up the recommended minimum cutoff voltage of a lipo pack for the sake of maximum pack longevity.

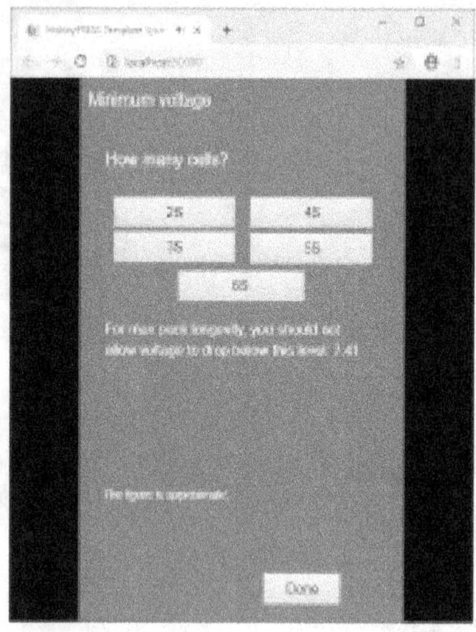

Heat is the largest enemy of your battery. Overcharging abuse is one easy way to overheat your battery. In theory, most battery cells have incorporated a protection mechanism against overcharging through increasing their ability to resist venting. However, heat is still generated along the process and is causing irreversible damage.

Smart Chargers using computer technology can perform step regulated charging techniques. They are expensive but are capable of tailoring charging current for rapid restoration of battery capacity due to the incorporation of controls for separating battery charging into finer stages.

    Copyright 2021. **The R.C.PRESS (Hong Kong)**. All rights reserved.

Thank you for reading. More RC books to come. For the latest updates please visit our website:

http :// r c p r e s s .c o m

If you are interested in 3D printing, we recommend this book, which talks about 3d modeling and printing in-depth: **http://rcpress.com/wp/?p=2379**

If you need to 3d print spare parts, give http://upgradeparts.com a try. There are many free vintage parts available over there.